Wine

THE DICTIONARY

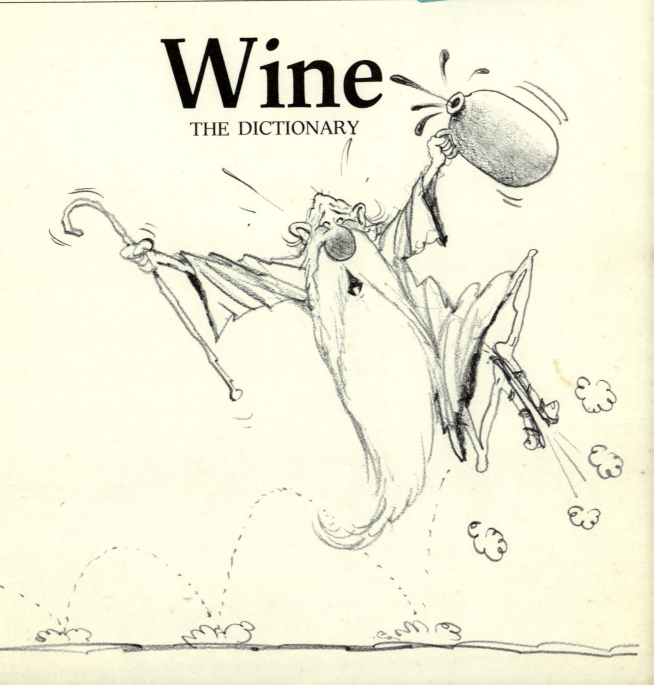

British Library Cataloguing in Publication Data

Dunstan, Keith
  Wine: the wine dictionary.
  1. Wine and wine making
  I. Title
  641.2'2'0207   TP548

  ISBN 0-7153-8824-X

© 1985 Text: Keith Dunstan
Illustrations: Jeff Hook

First published in Australia by Sun Books 1985
First published in Great Britain by David & Charles 1986

Printed in Great Britain
by Butler and Tanner Ltd   Frome
for David & Charles Publishers plc
Brunel House   Newton Abbot   Devon

Wine

THE WINE DICTIONARY
BY KEITH DUNSTAN
ILLUSTRATED BY JEFF HOOK

DAVID & CHARLES
Newton Abbot   London

ABSTAINER...

A

Abstainer	Human who generously leaves all the wine for non-abstainers.
Acid	Acid, not to be confused with sourness. Acid is a vital quality in wine. It gives it that tartness and grip, so necessary for longevity. Also a condition common in head waiters when the tip falls below 10 per cent.
Age	Many wines with the advancing years mellow, soften, take on infinite hues, glories and subtleties. Others never improve. They collapse and go to ruin. Wines are extraordinarily human.
Agreeable	Necessary technical term, akin to 'nice'. When your host serves you a dreary wine devoid of all style, character and taste, it is helpful to be able to roll your eyes to the ceiling: 'Mmmm, an agreeable wine, perhaps the most agreeable I have had this week'.
Aperitif	A French excuse for having a drink before you have the other drinks. *See* Liqueur.
Appellation Contrôlée	System laid down by law in France where wine-makers have to behave themselves. Labels on the bottles, for heaven's sake, must tell the truth. If a wine is made in Chablis, Burgundy, Bordeaux or Champagne then it must come from those districts. However if you live outside France it is not nearly such a problem. It is remarkable the Chablis, the Champagnes, the Burgundies that have turned up in the remotest corners of the USA and Australia.

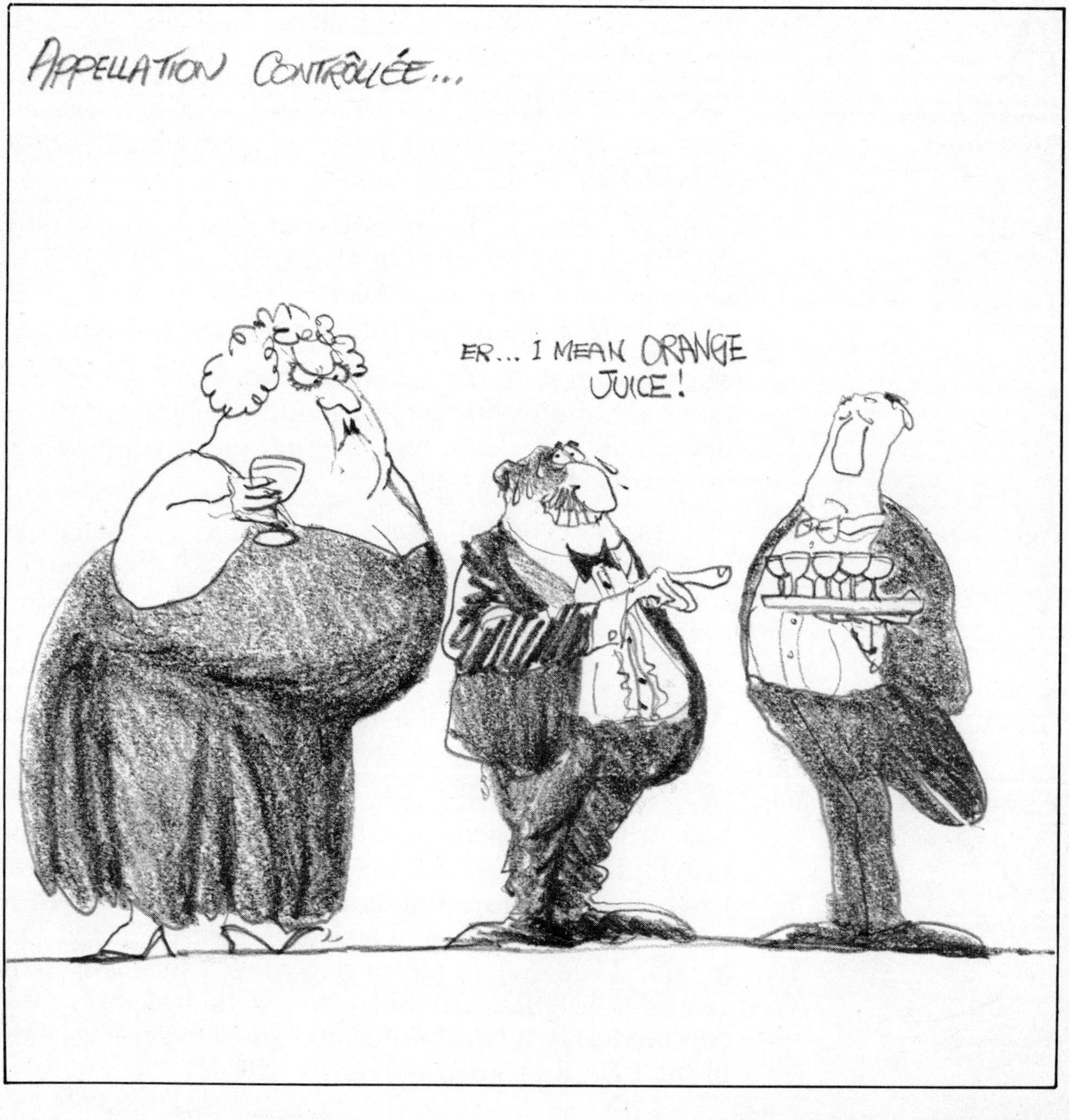
APPELLATION CONTRÔLÉE...
ER... I MEAN ORANGE JUICE!

Archbishop	An English mixed drink. Hot, sweetened wine in which floats an orange studded with cloves. After consuming six archbishops you get to meet the deity.
Au Revoir	You can talk about 'after taste', you can even describe that final, ultimate taste sensation as the 'farewell', ah, but if you describe it splendidly as the *au revoir* then all listeners will be convinced of your infinite knowledge.
Austere	Term applied to a stern, unyielding, not entirely friendly wine. Feeling of austerity sometimes can be improved by moving on to the third bottle.

B

Balance	Wonderful line to toss into a conversation when you don't know what to say about a wine. Say the wine has good 'balance'—it is sure to be balanced one way or another.
Balderdash	Mixture of liquors such as beer and wine or even wine and milk. It is also 99.999 per cent of almost everything that is spoken about wine.
Balloon	Device for filling with brandy which your wife steals for flower arrangements.
Barbarian	Worse than a thief, perjurer and wife beater. Doesn't bring out his best vintages when you come to dinner.

BALANCE...

Barbecue Red
A robust purple fluid which will not damage the top of the barbecue but of sufficient corrosive power to marry with the gristle of the carbonated chops and sausages.

Baume	One degree is equivalent to 1.8 per cent sugar. You hope that your loved one will be at least 55.5 per cent *baume* before the end of the evening.
Beads	The bubbles in a glass of wine, particularly Champagne. However, educated wine snobs always refer to beads. Bubbles is the name of the barmaid.
Beaujolais	A public relations ploy by the French. They have a race every year to get the first Beaujolais on to tables in London, San Francisco, New York and Sydney. It's your one chance to be proud that your wine is infinitely younger than your girlfriend.
Beaune	A great classic wine about which there is a classic story. A gentleman took his dog into the Savoy, sat down to lunch and told the waiter: 'I will have a bottle of Château Latour and would you kindly bring my dog a Beaune'.

BEAUNE...

Beerenauslese	Method in Germany where grapes are picked lovingly and individually as if they were roses or orchids. It is an ingenious method for pushing up the price to $60 a bottle.
Bin	Back in beautiful civilised, pre-discount times a bin was a cool dark area where one kept all the '45 d'Yquem, or maybe the '52 Latour. Now it is a cardboard box where the grocer has halved the price of all the junk he hasn't been able to sell for two years.

BIN...

Bin-Private

Same as previous entry, but now the grocer has discovered he can sell the stuff after all, he has put up the price by $2 a bottle.

BIN — PRIVATE

Birds

Dearly loved by M. Audubon, but hated by wine-growers. In vineyard wars they have tried everything to get rid of them: guns, artillery, electric wires, automatic machines that bark in the dawn, scarecrows, sirens. Ultimately the only answer is to grow more good Cabernet, Shiraz, Riesling, Chardonnay, Merlot and Pinot Noir than they can handle.

BIRDS...

VINEYARD
KEEP OUT
ALL BIRDS SHOT

Blanc de Blancs	You have one of these new-fangled corkscrews and you have just pushed the cork into the bottle.
Blend	The great art of the wine-maker is to be able to take a flavour from this vineyard, a nuance from that, just the perfect spice of acidity from over south, a touch of tannin from the north, and blend it all into the perfect wine. Actually it is a con-man's trick to disguise the fact that your superb Bordeaux came from a 5000-hectare plot in Algeria.
Blind Tasting	That peerless occasion when the bottles are all masked. Before an assembled audience you proceed to enunciate your remarkable skill, first divining the area, then the grape, then the year and even the label. You tell of its poor fruit, nondescript character, its flabbiness and disastrous future. Regrettably when they take off the wrapping it is the one you made or brought yourself.
Body	You can have a light body, a medium body or a full body, and that's the charming thing about wine, the full bodies usually come to one late in the evening.
Bottle	Smooth translucent receptacle which, mercifully, never will be replaced. Many females believe it is possible to give social judgement on the occupants of a house by the quality and style of their curtains. An infinitely more precise judgement can be made by the quality of the bottles they leave for the garbage man.

Bottle-Aged	Wine lover in his nineties. It is well known that good vintages inspire longevity.
Bouquet	In the full force of his eloquent romance with the grape the wine-lover detects the nuances of delicate and complex aromas—raspberries, mulberries, violets, the exotic breath of the iris, the rose, the geranium and even the gardenia. In the Hunter Valley of New South Wales they say a great Cabernet must have the overtones of a sweaty saddle. Less mundane people just enjoy the bloody stuff.
Boutique	Alternatively it could be called a hobby vineyard, and is no more than 5 or 10 hectares. An ingenious method by which doctors, dentists, shareholders and accountants convince the Taxation Department that this is an agricultural pursuit dedicated to the welfare of the nation.
Brandy	Useful aid in times of travail. The venerable Dr Johnson said: 'Claret is for boys, whisky is for men, but he who aspires to be a hero drinks brandy'.
Breathe	Breathing was all the go in the seventies. You would open your special bottle of vintage red four hours before the guests arrived. There it would be in a darkened room. 'What's that doing?' your wife would say. 'It's breathing', you would say enigmatically. Now there is much disagreement. Some connoisseurs think it is a mistake to give wine too much air. So your great Burgundy may only be allowed to gasp for breath for five minutes before serving.

BOTTLE-AGED...

Breath Tests	A great aid to the liberated female. Now 90 per cent of them have the evening control of automobiles.
Brink	That awful period when a wine is failing to improve, its youth is over, it is going to ruin. It is on the brink of death. You are on the brink yourself if it is a 1961 Latour and you have another 11 of them in the cupboard.

BREATH TESTS

BUFF...

Buff	One who knows how to handle the plastic tap on a wine cask.
Burgundy	In Australia it's almost the opposite to what it is in France. In Ockerland your Burgundy-type is a big luscious, gutsy wine. In France is it the joyous product of Burgundy in eastern France. The reds very often are Pinot Noir, delicate, clean. No doubt the French eventually will discover what they are doing.
BYOG	An indigenous Australian term which bites deep into the national ethos. An insurance policy: you bring your own grog.

C

Cabernet	The greatest grape of all. The nice people learn to roll it off the tongue . . . Cab-air-nay . . . or for some . . . Car-bur-nay. It is 'in' to be able to talk of the smell of blackcurrants, or in Australia, blackberries. Old Cabernets take on a cigar-box nose. It is an expensive little grape, so it tends to be a good mixer, with Shiraz, with Merlot, with Malbec, with almost everything except Schweppes.
Carbon Dioxide	Useful non-toxic gas. An anonymous scientist who is still waiting to receive his Nobel prize invented the ingenious system 'Methode Carbondioxoise' by which Champagne with superb CO_2 can be produced for $1.20 a bottle.
Cask	Once a work of art, an exquisite thing, made by a cooper, each stave warped into a perfect elipse so all comes together to make a barrel in which noble wine is delicately matured. Now a cask is made of plastic and it is filled only with wine that no wine-maker ever thought fit for putting in a cask.
Cave	French word for cellar. As Fitzgerald almost said: 'A bottle of wine, a blonde, and a cave'.

Cellar	There is only one way to do it. $P = 2C(Y+X)$. That is, your wine purchases must be double the capacity of both yourself and your friends. It is the only way you get the strength of character to have bottles that live beyond an early youth.
Cellar Book	Those who are deep into the mania keep a record, a log of purchases. They enter wines in, they enter wines out, complete with chart. The ultimate *coup de grace* is to be able to say to your guests as you extract the cork: 'Oh yes, I see that I bought a dozen of this at twenty-two and six a bottle. Today you would have to pay . . .'
Chablis	Little town south-east of Paris in the department of Yonne. The small surrounding district produces some of the most famous of all white Burgundies. It can be made only from the Chardonnay grape and they are lucky if they produce 800 000 gallons a year. By an extraordinary coincidence one sees Chablis in munificent quantity in liquor stores all the way from downtown Los Angeles to downtown Melbourne. In its ultimate refined glory it comes in 4-gallon plastic bags.
Champagne	Name of a wine-producing area in north-eastern France, famed for glorious sparkling wines of the finest quality. Amazing what they can do in many other places using the same name with local juice plus carbon dioxide.
Chardonnay	A trendy grape variety in California, New Zealand and Australia which the French have been fiddling with for about 300 years.

CELLAR

CHÂTEAU...

Château	Usually a little winery with galvanised iron walls and roof at the end of an umade track. There is a sign out 'Not Open to Visitors on Sundays'. They appear in the most remarkable places, even Australia, with titles of great nobility like Château Downunda.
Cheating	It helps at blind tastings to spot the evidence. For example, the sight of a label or the shape of a bottle is worth 50 years of experience.

Cheerful

You must appreciate that wines take on human characteristics. You can have cheerful wines; or sullen, gloomy wines that are strangely reticent on the middle palate. You can have pathetic wines that are lacking in backbone; or subtle wines full of great mystery. They can be eloquent, charming. They can be nervous, but then again they can be supple, ripe, full of generosity, and superbly well rounded. Sometimes you don't know whether to drink them or take them to bed.

CLEARING THE PALATE...

Clearing the Palate	That wondrous, educated piece of equipment, your palate, can't just be rushed into action. Like a Lamborghini with 12 cylinders and 24 carburettors it needs warming before it can give peak performance. You clear it first, a dry biscuit, a nibble of bread, a prayer to Bacchus. This is why you see so few anorexic wine-lovers.
Coarse	Drinking your wine out of a cup. Unbelievably coarse: using a straw.
Cognac	Brandy made from the area around the town of Cognac. That and Armagnac are almost the only French names that have not received the honour of being copied everywhere on the globe.

Colour

It is essential that you get your performance absolutely right. Don't just rush in and crudely start drinking. You get points for being the slowest and most circumspect. Contemplate your glass for a moment, taking in the exquisite scene. Hold it by the stem or base, raise it to your nose and give a meaningful 'ahhh'. Then inspect it for colour, *not* by holding it to the light. Oh dear no, the light source could be misleading. You hold it low, against a white table cloth, hence you get the exact nuance of shade for your expert eye. Any time now you will be able to take a sip.

Colour...

Complex	When you haven't the slightest idea of the origin of the wine, do toss in the word complex. 'A fascinating wine, full of complex nuances, and esters. Bound to last.' It is certain to last until you finish the bottle anyway.
Consumption	The theory of consumption or the law of diminishing returns was invented by wine-lover, drinker and *bon viveur*, Len Evans. He claims that he drinks a bottle of wine a day. He has, on his reckoning, only 20 years left to live. Therefore he has a miserable remaining 7000 bottles to enjoy. (We have added a few bottles for celebratory days.) This means with so little left to drink every bottle must be a joy, a marvel and never *vin ordinaire*.
Cooking Wine	'Oh darling, why didn't you tell me? I thought it was just an old one you didn't want.'
Cork	Initial barrier between imbiber and imbibed, first step between hope and glory.
Corkage	There is a famous story of a man who was charged corkage when he took his wife to a bawdy house. The same hideous system applies when you take your own bottle to a restaurant.
Côte d'Or	The home of the great Burgundies. One dreams of Romanée-Conti, Chambolle-Musigny, Nuits-St-Georges, Meursault, Montrachet . . . Translated it means the Golden Slope. It could mean the delightful way that the ridges trap the sun. On the other hand it could mean what you have to pay for the darned stuff.

Cream Sherry	What Aunty gives you with cream cake. They match perfectly.
Crust	This is the sludge, the potassium tartate deposited particularly by grand old reds and vintage Ports. The greatest sin is to disturb the crust while the wine is being decanted. There is the famous story of the waiter at the bush hotel who brought forward an old bottle. 'Did you shake it?' said the wine-lover nervously. 'No Sir, but I WILL! I WILL!'

CORK...

D

Dead Marine
A cadaver. Some citizens collect the empties of great wines they have consumed. But keeping old bottles is like having pictures of past wives and mistresses; an exercise of tragedy, of past love and joys. Optimism and hope is a full bottle.

DEAD MARINE...

Decant	This is great stuff at a dinner party. Not only does it give you an opportunity to turn on an acting performance that would do credit to Laurence Olivier, but also the guests cannot fail to admire and see the label on the bottle. For best results take the bottle into another room and spend 15 minutes in slowly extracting the cork so that the contents will not be disturbed. Then with beautiful co-ordination decant the wine into an illustrious antique decanter. Using the light of a strong electric bulb? Certainly not, you always decant with a candle held close to the neck of the bottle.
Dessert Wine	The mythical question is always asked, what books, what wine would you require when stranded on a desert island. The greatest wine of all, clearly, is Château d'Yquem and I would require at least 100 cases. It would then become a dessert island.
Distinguished	Exceptional character, style and breeding. Usually it is a term that you apply to the head waiter.
Domestic	It couldn't be any good. It was grown locally. *See* Imported.
Dom Pérignon	Clever fellow who is credited with inventing Champagne, *circa* 1670. According to legend he tasted the first marvellous drop and said: 'I am drinking stars'. Seeing stars the next day is another matter.
Doughnut	When a wine has a good foretaste and a brilliant aftertaste but nothing in the middle, it is said to be a doughnut wine. The big danger is always to look for the hole and never the doughnut.

DRUNK...

Drunk	A wine-lover is never drunk. He merely becomes fortified.
Dry	Almost everything associated with the grape means something else. Like the law it is designed deliberately to confuse. Dry doesn't mean dry, just as *brut* doesn't mean brute. Both mean without sweetness, which doesn't mean that they are sour either. The first 10 000 bottles are the most difficult to understand.

Dumb...

Dumb　　Useful term for when the wine has absolutely nothing to say. Sometimes you wish it could be applied also to the drinkers.

E

Epicurean	Fearless, devoted creature, who refuses to be diverted from dedicated path by weight watchers, wowsers, vegetarians or diet gurus like Nathan Pritikin and Robert Atkins. Nothing diverts him from his desire to fill his stomach only with choicest foods and finest vintages.
Estates	If you can't get away with calling your tax-dodge vineyard a 'château', at least you can call it an 'estate', say, the Bacchus Estate. It means a little property on which you owe half a million to the bank.
Euphoria	It is said that marathon runners frequently reach an ethereal high. It comes after 30 or 40 kilometres, a period when they feel they can run on for ever. Wine-lovers hit it after three-quarters of a bottle.

F

Fermentation	Even before he discovered the wheel prehistoric man stumbled across something very peculiar, the sugar in grape juice converted into alcohol; humble juices became wine. This tended to make life bearable for the next 50 000 years.

FERMENTATION...

Finesse	Another glorious word to toss in when you are not too sure what you are talking about. 'This wine has *finesse* . . .' Maybe the real *finesse* was shown by the wine-maker. He was wearing a clean shirt when they started crushing the grapes.
Finish	You get the beginning, then you get those delicate and interesting flavours on the middle palate, and ultimately you get 'the finish'. In the very best and most eloquent circles it is always called 'the farewell'. Actually the most remarkable farewell is the flavour you get on your tongue about nine o'clock the following morning.

FIRST GROWTH (SEE ALSO 'FLABBY')...

First Growth	Or *premier cru*. Back in 1855 the French Chamber of Commerce asked the Bordeaux Syndicate of Wine Brokers to give a list of the best Bordeaux wines. Four reds which received the honour of being first growth were Lafite-Rothschild, Margaux, Latour and Haut-Brion. The only first growth most of us see is around the waistline.
Flabby	Good term to use when the dear old thing hasn't got any acid, hasn't got any tannin, hasn't got any fruit but has got lots of glumph. Good flab comes easily to wine-lovers. There are 100 calories in every glass.
Foot Crushing	Classic, traditional method for making wine. There is a drawback. It turns white feet to an interesting shade of vermilion. Best to wear shoes to parties for several weeks afterwards.
Free Run	Getting in with your own bottles without being nailed by the wine waiter.
Fumé-Blanc	Trendy term for white wine in which the maker is saying 'I'm not too damn sure what it is'.

FOOT CRUSHING...

G

Glass	Don't hang on to it with your fist around its belly. Don't even hold it by its stem. Take it by the base, delicately hold its platform with your thumb and forefinger and with great elegance take it up to your nose. Immediately they will think you know something about it, even that you are a Chevalier du Tastevin. *See* Society.
Gluhwein	Hot, spicy winter wine. Makes coarse young reds drinkable and snow bunnies lovable.

GRIP...

Grip	The opposite of anaemic, flabby or spineless. Look for a young Algerian red or a Hungarian Bull's Blood or an ouzo and you will experience a grip like that of a Greek weight-lifter.
Gutsy	When the wine is big, majestic, purple, as loaded with tannin as a military boot. When it's only fit for a steel-lined gut. It's gutsy.

H

Hangover	There is a theory that if the wine is of great quality and you only drink first growths you never get a hangover. Actually there is no known cure, except perhaps a glass of Champagne at 11 am. The Germans have a much more evocative name for hangover, *Katzenjammer*.
Headache	Curious pain one gets in the head the next day, never from the wine. It comes from the concentration and worry over which bottle to open.

Head and Shoulders	Sensitive term for a eunuch of a wine. Magnificent nose, splendid appearance up top but when you get down to where things really happen nothing's there.
Heavenly Choirs	Legend has it that when finally you discover the perfect wine, you hear the heavenly choirs and angels begin to sing. It is also time to take a taxi home.
Hermitage	How grateful we should be to the Church. Legend has it hermits took Shiraz grapes from Iran and propagated them in the Hermitage district of the Rhône Valley. Depending how up-market you are the wine is called Hermitage or Shiraz. For example, New South Wales under the influence of the Hunter River prefers Hermitage, whereas the rest of Australia sinks to mere Shiraz.
Hock	An English term for wines from the Rhine region of Germany, but with a enthusiasm in labelling it can mean any damn wine on earth.
Home Bottler	He gets his wine by the hogshead from an old mate. He uses re-cycled corks, puts it into old Sherry or even turpentine bottles. He has his own marvellous cute labels and the vicar likes him because he sells it at the church fête. He believes his rough red is superb, equal to the stuff bottled professionally using the most modern technical methods by the dull old hands who have been doing it for 150 years.
Honest	Something which doesn't normally apply to the label, but is a beautifully handy term to apply to a wine that is decent, pure, well behaved, but like the archbishop's daughter, doesn't do much else.

I

Ice	Hideous translucent adulterant that comes in cubes, particularly favoured by Americans. Treat with care, should never be allowed in contact with quality wine.
Imbibe	Some taste, some sip, some drink, some gulp, but the utterly trendy imbibe.
Imported	A belief that it is always better if it came from elsewhere. *See* Domestic.
Inverse Snob	One who despises pretty scenes of French châteaux on his casks or flagons.
In Vino Veritas	An old saying that in wine there is truth. In other words the truth only comes out after the third bottle. Actually we never see it that way. The third bottle is when the old winos start telling their monstrous lies.
Irrigation	Villainous term. The great vineyards depend upon natural rainfall. When you irrigate it is best to do it at night when nobody is looking.

J

Judge	One who can hit a sawdust bucket at 15 paces.
Judgement	Great judgement is being able to gauge how much wine to lay down for your old age. André Simon was perhaps the greatest gourmet and wine-lover of his age. His judgement was magnificent. Legend has it that on the day of his death only one bottle remained in his cellar.

K

Keg	A nice charming little barrel, usually under 10 gallons, the sort to tide you over the week-end.

L

Label	Sheet of paper designed to mystify the purchaser. Some labels contain every conceivable item of information from the name of the vigneron's aunty down to the moment of conception of the grape. Indeed they tell you so much about the wine there is no need to drink it. Generally, the quantity of information on the label is in inverse proportion to the quality of the wine.

Lacrima Christi	The most beautifully named of all wines. The tear of Christ. It is a slightly sweet wine that is produced on the foothills of Mt Vesuvius. One can only presume that Christ's tear had to be one of joy.
Larynx	Item at the back of the throat that suffers from dehydration and needs vinous irrigation.
Late Picking	The later you pick your grapes the sweeter the juice. One wonders whether it also applies to brides.
Legs	A term for the little globules which fall down the side of a glass when you swirl a splendid, rich wine. However after several glasses you often see a better variety.
Liebfraumilch	In translation, mother's milk. Not quite as life sustaining as the real thing, but the world-wide sales of this German blended white are so great that it must unquestionably have healing, curative and soul-soothing qualities.
Limpid	Clear, beautiful, with outstanding brightness, like the blue eyes of the young Elizabeth Taylor.
Liqueur	An excuse for having another drink when you have drunk everything else. *See* Aperitif.
Look	You must appreciate that one never 'drinks' a wine. When you are interested in a vintage say that you would like to 'see' it, or even better, you would like to 'look' at it. Vignerons appreciate these subtleties.

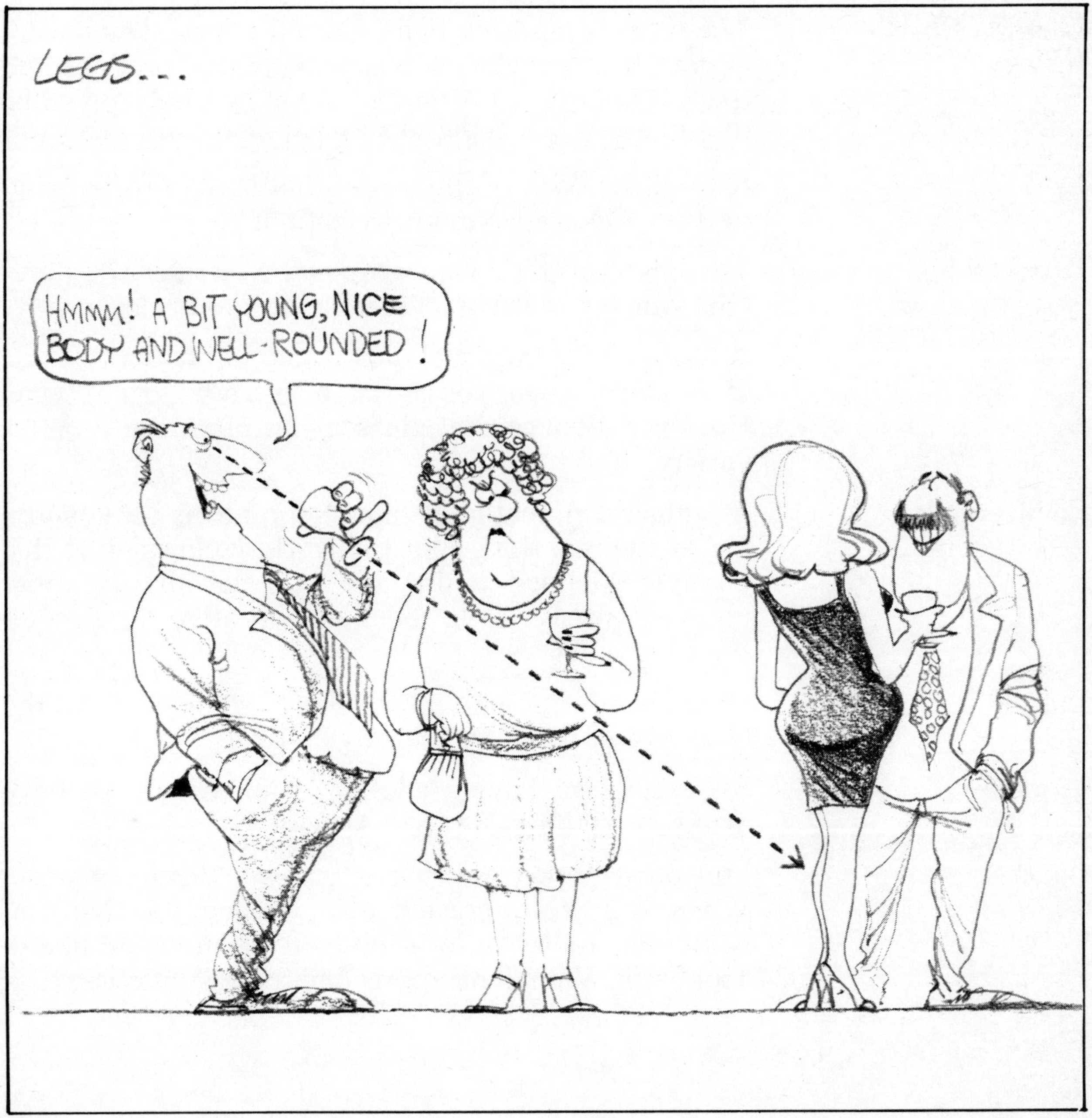
LEGS...
HMMM! A BIT YOUNG, NICE BODY AND WELL-ROUNDED!

M

Machiavelli	A Florentine statesman, whose name has become the epitome of unscrupulous intrigue. However his estate at Percussina produces a quite splendid Chianti so all is forgiven.
Madeira	By tradition the arch seducer of young maidens. Alas, by the time you have consumed a 'small cask' of the stuff, the seducer is no longer seductible.

MADEIRA...

MEDICINE FACE...

Magnum	Double-sized bottle. Designed specifically for the wine-lover when doctors and wives order him to drink only a bottle a day.
Marriage	One marries wine to food. Could one suggest an interesting Gewürtztraminer with the smoked salmon; a fine Sémillon with the trout; a great Cabernet Sauvignon with the *filet de boeuf* and a Trockenbeeren-auslese with the *crêpes suzettes*. Wine marriage is only 10 per cent as tricky as human marriage.
Mark-Up	The extraordinary manner in which wine bottles gather value as soon as they pass through a restaurant door. Sometimes the mark-up is as high as 500 per cent.
Medicine Face	Try to look happy when your dear friend brings out the flagon and tells you it is just as good as the stuff you get in the bottle at four times the price. That pained wince as you raise your glass to your lips is known technically as medicine face.
Mellow	Start with the gentle innocent whites, move to the flowery Burgundies, then on to the glorious robust reds. Mellow is that soft, ripe, well-matured feeling that comes with the eloquent Sauternes and then the Port. It is a feeling close to divinity.
Memory	Wine-lovers should have total recall for colour, taste, nose. They should remember all their great wine experiences. They may not remember the names of their children, or even remember that they dined with the Molyneux-Smiths in March 1964; but of course they remember that they had Château Latour '58 with the beef, and the '54 Château d'Yquem with the dessert was an event even greater than their marriage the previous year.

METHUSELAH...

Methuselah	A marvellous Biblical gentleman who lived to be 969 years old. Allegedly a receptacle for eight bottles of Champagne. However not nearly as marvellous as Nebuchadnezzar who lived for only 43 years and is a receptacle for 20 bottles of Champagne.
Mis en Bouteille au Château . . .	Nobody else would bottle the bloody stuff for us.
Must	The newly pressed grape juice ready for fermentation. It is also the wifely look you get across the dinner table at 11.30 pm when you are pondering the bliss of another glass of vintage Port.
Mystique	The system of cleverly enshrouding wine-drinking in mystery by using terms your fellow drinkers don't understand.

N

Nervous Reflex	Shocking condition which strikes a wine-lover when he is deprived of the grape at meals. His hand keeps reaching out for a glass that is not there.
Neutral	Doesn't belong to the left, doesn't belong to the right, doesn't express any opinions. The sort of wine that they serve in carafes at the club.

Noah	Zoo manager, ship owner and builder (among his lesser accomplishments). He also ran a vineyard for three and a half centuries and very sensibly never drank water. He believed that it tasted of sinners. After all, so many terrible people drowned in it.
Noble Rot	The French have an even more noble term, *pourriture noble* and the technical description is *botrytis cinerea*. It is a grey mould which forms on grapes after a long summer, coupled with cool weather, humidity and wondrous fogs. The French are cleverer at securing *botrytis* weather than anyone else on earth. It is devilish hard to score in California, impossible in Spain and rare enough in Australia. When it arrives the wine-growers offer tears of joy. *Botrytis* grapes are picked lovingly, even individually and their sugar content is magnificent. It is the stuff of the great Sauternes like d'Yquem and Suduiraut. Noble rot could also describe much of the talk at wine dinners.
Non-Vintage	If the wine-maker thinks his wine is top drawer then he will have the year of the vintage on his bottle. On the other hand he could be crafty and blend a top year with a not-so-good. Maybe it is just a wine from a lesser paddock. These are non-vintage wines. Many of the great ladies of the screen and stage do not reveal their age, but that doesn't mean they are not good company.
Nose	Should be angular and pointed for placing in tasting glasses. A good nose should mature in the glass. After saturation on several thousand occasions it should change colour to a warm, lovable shade of vermilion.

O

Oak	Wondrous things can be done to a wine by allowing it to linger in oak casks. The devoted wine-maker can spend like a mad punter in acquiring costly Limousin oak, French oak, Spanish oak, American oak, Baltic oak or even she-oak. But it is amazing what some do on a dark night with some wood shavings or a good pencil sharpener.
Oenologist	One who has much scientific knowledge about wine and out-oens everyone else.
Oloroso	Old, rich, mellow and semi-sweet. Can be tapped to excellent advantage.
Over the Hill	Most of the young whites are gone after a decade, nearly all the reds are getting shaky at 20, good Cabernets might make it to 40 or 50 years. You can shoot most footballers by the time they are 30, drown tennis players at 35, and purge cricketers and base-ballers utterly at 40. Mistresses pick up very few deals after middle-age. But there is a wonderful thing about wine-drinking. Taste is the last thing to go. Some wine-drinkers at 100 are still not over the hill.
Oxidised	It was given to you on your birthday in 1955. You have kept it for 30 years waiting for a moment of sufficient grandeur to open it. You take quarter of an hour to extract the cork for fear it might crumble. Horror. The lovely thing has perished and smells like vinegar; a tragedy akin to the death of your own mother.

OENOLOGIST...

P

Palate	One starts off as a tender young creature when all wines have a beauty and richness. Then you acquire that mysterious gift, a palate. You start looking for subtlety, perfection and you discover that 90 per cent of the world's wine is not fit for consumption. Gone for you are the generous flagons, the wonderfully convenient casks, with their plastic taps always at the ready on the sideboard. As your palate improves and becomes more skilled, satisfaction is only to be found in the *premiers crus* and the great years. A palate is an expensive and lonely acquisition.
Paul	Saint. Died AD 67. Apostle who by legend was not devoted to women but deserves eternal praise. In a letter to his friend Timothy he said: 'Drink no longer water, but use a little wine for thy stomach's sake and thine often infirmities.'
Perfume	The most hideous crime is to wear it to a wine-tasting. No perfume even from the great houses of Paris has the divine fragrance of a great white Burgundy or a lovely old Cabernet.
Plonk	One can be a plonko, a plonk artist, a plonk merchant, or a plonk dot. It is an extremely economic approach to wine.

Pop	Vulgar noise made by an untamed Champagne cork. The correct upmanship with a bottle of Champagne is to show that, really, you do this every day. So you wrap the top with a clean white towel, hold the bottle at 45 degrees, and extract the cork by turning the bottle (not the cork) as silently as possible, as if you were doing it in church.
Port	A shelter, a home, a haven against storm and tempest. A noble Port wine should serve a similar service. A vintage Port should be aged in the bottle and 10 to 15 years old. It is the English custom to pass the decanter round the table from right to left, another outrageous plot against the left-hander.
Precocious	All creatures, bottled and unbottled, who have developed with an unhealthy rapidity. Try again and select another item that has matured more tenderly and gracefully.
Pressings	There is the wine produced from the juice which runs freely from the crushed fruit. Ah, but then there are also the pressings when the bejabbers are pressed out of the so-called *pomace*. The free-run wine often is sold separately as the superior vintage, but then there are old hands who can talk of great wines made from pressings, rich and elegant in flavour. Dammit, you could stand up a fork in some of them.

POP...

Prickle　　　　Some curious and quite remarkable scientific instruments have been invented but there are still some wonderful wine-makers who believe the best method for testing the progress of fermentation is to put your arm deep into the vat and feel the prickle on the warm flesh. It is known as bubblemanship.

PRICKLE (SEE ALSO 'RED NED')...

Purple   The colour of fresh vibrant youth . . . 'I would suggest, Sir, that this is a young wine.' Young? Hell, they made it last Tuesday.

S

Sacramental Wines	In the words of wine writer, Walter James, the purveyors of altar wine almost invariably are stronger in theology than oenology.
Sawdust	Wood powder, placed in bucket, essential to maintain the sobriety of the dedicated wine-taster. Its degree of saturation is in inverse proportion to the quality of the wine to be tasted.

SACRAMENTAL WINES...

Schloss	German equivalent of château, or castle, and it is quite untrue that the people who inhabit them get *schlossed*.
Screwtop	Hideous modern aberration, as shocking as the clip-on bow tie or the plastic rose. Instead of the divine POP, there is a mere PHUT.
Send Back	Act of fearless courage, worthy of Victoria Cross or Congressional Medal of Honor. Looking directly into the cold eyes of the head waiter and saying: 'This will not do'.

SEND BACK...

Sensuous	Very popular term with wine-lovers. It means rich, smooth, opulent, seductive. However those who use it should pursue some other activity.
Shiraz	A city in south-west Iran near the Persian Gulf. It gave its name to the best known wine grape, but they'll cut your hand off if you drink it there. *See* Hermitage.
Show Wines	You sweat, take care, pick your grapes as if they were diamonds for a loved one. After pressing there is eternal vigilance. You watch the temperature day and night, as if worrying over a crying baby. You put it in your best oak, maturing in small casks. You send off four bottles with signed authority that you have 500 gallons. Lo, it wins the medal for the best red at the Grand Panjandrum Show. Then you declare your triumph with a special label on the 100 000 cases that you sell for the next ten years.
Smoking	There are crimes too awful to contemplate; drinking a *premier cru* out of a crockery cup; selling wine in an aluminium can; (shudder) putting sugar into a crisp Riesling; pushing a cork into a vintage wine because you can't find a corkscrew; shaking an old bottle. But all these are as nothing compared with the Philistine who smokes while you are drinking fine wine.
Smooth	Usually the head waiter and his degree of smoothness is in direct proportion to the terrifying prices on the wine list.
Snob	A creature who always opens his bottles using a clean white napkin and turns the label towards the guests.

Society	Once you become the complete wine nut there is no turning back—you join a society, like the Beefsteak and Burgundy Club, the Wine and Food Society, or terribly august French organisations like La Chaine des Rôtisseurs or La Confrèrie des Chevaliers du Tastevin. Dinner takes about four hours and the names of the wines are more important than the names of the people present.
Soft	Pleasing finish without being hard or aggressive. A condition you try to find amongst wine-dealers.
Sommelier	Magnificently up-market name for a wine waiter. By tradition he should have a fancy costume, a big silver chain around his neck, a tasting cup, a decorated apron and know more about wine than even the critic of *The Times*. If he is splendid enough he could be worth even 30 per cent on the wine prices.
Sunday	Usually a sacred day at the vineyard. The proprietor hopes desperately to be alone with his family.

T

Table Wine	Remarkable generic term for wine. The wines you have to be careful of are the under-the-table wines.
Tangy	Rich, spicy, with a zestful bouquet. Term invented by a copy writer for TV commercials.

Tanker   Magnificent device for converting one wine area into another. In France tankers convert homely Algerian wines into noble Bordeaux wines. In Australia tankers help the bulk of Barossa convert to the purest of Hunter River greats and in California tankers can achieve miracles by converting generous fruit from the San Joaquin Valley into glories from the Napa.

TANKER ...

Tart	Said to be high in acid, but tarts, with a little coddling, fondling, and keeping in dark places, can become beautiful and lovable.
Taste Buds	Small items on the tongue and soft palate which flash messages to the brain. The true taste buddy rolls the wine round his tongue like water in a lavatory cistern.
Tastevin	A tasting cup of silver or pewter to hang on a ribbon round one's neck. It's very handy. One might lose one's spectacles but *never* one's wine receptacle.
Taut	Firm, severe, unyielding, like the wine merchant's demands for payment.
Tawny	Red to brownish upon maturation. With a bit of luck you will find her as the evening progresses.
Tax	Noble, unselfish contribution which the wine-drinker makes to the glory of his government. He knows that with every glass he drinks he is helping to keep a fighter aircraft aloft and a public servant in employment.
Teetotaller	'All the great villainies of history, from the murder of Abel onward, have been perpetrated by sober men, and chiefly by teetotallers. But all the charming things, from the "Song of Songs" to bouillabaisse, and from the nine Beethoven symphonies to the Martini cocktail, have been given to humanity by men who, when the hour came, turned from tap water to something with colour to it, and more in it than mere oxygen and hydrogen.' H. L. Mencken.

Temperature	It varies according to national custom. Both Americans and Australians are passionate about refrigeration. In Australia they will even freeze the glasses. Whites should be cool, reds mostly are happier at room temperature. However there is one golden rule—the more villainous the wine, the colder it should be. It helps to kill the taste.
Thin	Opposite of big. Requires more body. Only cure a course of calorie-charged white Burgundies and great reds that have developed profundity and corporation.

THIN...

Threshold
This is the level at which first you can detect the quality of the wine. Some utterly skilled creatures can tell just by looking at the colour or sniffing the bouquet. I mean with enough practice you mightn't have to drink the stuff at all.

THRESHOLD ...

Thurber	James. The man who made the ultimate comment on wine. As a caption for one of his *New Yorker* cartoons he wrote: 'It's a naïve domestic Burgundy without any breeding, but I think you'll be amused by its presumption'.
Travel	Wines travel well or they travel badly. There's the famous story of an English vigneron who produced a wine for a French visitor. The Englishman produced his bottle of brilliant red and said proudly: 'I want you to know this wine was produced on that hill over there'. 'Didn't travel well, did it?' said the Frenchman.
Tulip	Delightfully shaped tasting glass, broad at the waist, narrow at the lip. By anthropological progression wine-drinkers eventually will acquire sharp noses so that they will fit into tasting glasses.
Tun	A very large vat of wine, a tun of conviviality and pleasure.

Tulip ...

U

Unbalanced	It doesn't hang together, too much fruit maybe, too much acid, not enough tannin. It is shaky and unstable, like the slow walk to bed.
Unripe	Put her away for a while, keep her in a dry place, in a darkened room at the right temperature, and she will come good.

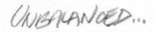

V

Vigneron	He puts up with bush fire, hail, drought, rain when he doesn't want it, phylloxera, downy mildew; governments use him mercilessly as a tax resource, citizens invade his property seven days a week. However his service to mankind is great. Nobody wants to know him in an off-year, but in a great year he is the most loved creature on earth.
Vinegar	The house wine.
Vinicide	Worse than homicide—drinking a wine before it is ready.
Vintage	Year of birth. There are good years, mediocre years and terrible years. There's the delightful story of the elderly wine-lover lover who was offered a bottle of the year of his birth. Charmingly he asked for a 1952 which was a quite marvellous year in Bordeaux. *See* Non-Vintage.
Vintage Card	The right people carry vintage cards. This enables them to run an eye over a wine list with perfect knowledge of the good and bad years. The ultimate snob however is the gentleman who knows the perfect, little-known wine that is a triumph in an off-year, then takes 30 minutes telling how he found out.

W

Waiter Creature who can read a customer better than a wine label. Knows how to stand with a face as impassive as a Russian premier when his customers thinks a Fumé-Blanc is something you smoke or a Sew-turn is what he should be drinking with fish. But patience is his trade. When a rich guest orders a Montrachet of a good year he hopes they will leave just a little for him.

WAITER ...

Water	Lady at Dinner Party: 'You mean to tell me that you never, never, let water touch your lips? Then what do you use to clean your teeth, pray?' Retired Major: 'A light Sauternes, madam.' Anon.
Weeper	Regrettable seepage. Condition extraordinarily common amongst Australian politicians and sportsmen.
Weingut	Wine estate in Germany. In English-speaking countries it is that expensive and beautifully developed corporation that goes under the watchchain.
Well-Made	The vigneron's daughter.
Wine	The cleverest thing God invented after sex. Wine lasts longer and causes infinitely less trouble.

WEEPER ...

WINE

Wineabout	Technical term for wine enthusiast who has map of vineyards which are open to the public. Starting with those whose doors open at 10 am he can manage to fit in six to eight vineyards a day. He is particularly fascinated with the tasting room. There he starts with the Rieslings and wends his way through the reds to the Ports, voicing his enthusiasm over each to the vigneron. Sometimes he actually buys a bottle.
Wine List	Beautiful array of wines—Gothic script, parchment paper, gloriously presented in leather-bound cover—all of which you can have at home for a quarter the price.
Wino	Human addicted to the grape. Like addiction to golf and fishing, adoration of old steam engines and even cricket, there's no known cure.
Wine Rape	Similar to vinicide but more serious. Drinking a great wine long before it is ready. It is not a capital offence, but almost.

X

Xeres	The old name for the Spanish town of Jerez, which, some think, gave its name to Sherry and you couldn't get a better excuse for using the letter X.